A Book of Poems
About a
Nurse Crying
with and for
Her Patients

A Book of Poems About a Nurse Crying

with and for

Her Patients

Florida Arianna Pearl

Library of Congress Control Number: 2017918365
ISBN: Hardcover   978-1-5434-6692-8
             Softcover   978-1-5434-6693-5
             eBook   978-1-5434-6694-2

Print information available on the last page.

Rev. date: 12/05/2017

To order additional copies of this book, contact:
Xlibris
1-888-795-4274
www.Xlibris.com
Orders@Xlibris.com
770279

CONTENTS

ABOUT THE AUTHOR

Florida Arianna Pearl (pen name),
lived in South Carolina. She grew up
poor and deprived of loving parents.
She would later go on to finish
college and use her life experiences
to write poetry and short stories of
the different experiences she lived
through at home, work, and school
and through her search for mental healing.

ROOM 711

I was only twenty-one years old. I had been married for two years to a young twenty-two-year-old engineer. My husband had just completed his education, and I had been out of nursing school for a year. New in the nursing profession, my husband and I were happy because we had just learned from my obstetrician that we were three months pregnant. We were trying to find a name suitable for our first child.

On January 2, 1960, I was six months pregnant and had just been promoted to head nurse of the cardiovascular unit at Francis Doctor Hospital. My first admission was a middle-aged female. She was so beautiful. She had long brown hair that was well arranged. She was well kept and seemed in excellent physical condition. She stated, "I am here to have a small varicose vein removed from my left leg. Doctor Bell told me, I will have the surgery tomorrow morning at eight o'clock and should be back in my room by nine that same morning and free to leave the hospital in two or three days."

1

I lamented, "At least we know that you will only be here a few days. Let me show you to your room."

A nice handsome middle-aged man was with her. The middle-aged man had black hair. He was about six feet tall. He walked up from behind her and stood near her right side. He proceeded to hold her hand. She said, "This is my beloved husband, George."

I proceeded to take them to room 711. I assisted her to get undressed in the bathroom into the hospital gown. I escorted her to the bed. I sent our best nurse aide into her room after I left the room to assist her if needed. I thought, *I have not seen such a beautiful middle-aged female in my entire life.* It was nearing time for me to get off work.

The patient in room 711 left for vascular surgery at 0800 hours; at 1000 hours, I noticed that she had not returned from surgery. At 1500 hours, nearing time for me to be relieved, she returned from surgery. Upon checking her records, while the surgical technician took her to her room to put her to bed, I read from doctor's notes that her right leg had been amputated. She arrested on the operating table, and after CPR was done to bring her back to life, she developed gas gangrene in the right leg, causing it to have to be removed to save her life. Her husband signed for the surgery. Two days later, her left leg was blue, and the doctors requested to remove it, but she refused to sign for another surgery.

About a week later, her body was blue-black from her toes up to her waist. We did not change her bottom linen for fear that turning her body could rip her apart. We washed her face, brushed her hair, gave her oral care, and changed her top linen and pillowcase. An automatic air room freshener was placed into her room to prevent smelling the foul odor from the dead tissue of her body. She was medicated every two to three hours with morphine to prevent pain. Two days later, I entered her room to give her an injection of morphine. I mistakenly asked her, "How do you feel?" I asked all my patients this question out of habit.

Her room was filled with roses, red and white roses her husband had bought for her. She said, "Come in and take a rose for yourself. I have such a lovely husband and, and he loves me so much, and I love him dearly. We have no children but life has been good to both of us."

She went on to say, "I feel fine, dear." I was in disbelief. She must have heard my thoughts. She said, "Honey, I have had a good life, I know my condition, don't worry about me, my life has

been better than many, I enjoyed the good, and I accept the bad."
Looking at her body wasting away, I could only hope that if I found
myself in a similar condition, that I could be as strong as she had
been. She lay there when her body was wasting away.

The following morning, the director of nurses sent me to the fifth
floor because the head nurse on that floor was ill, and there was
not even a charge nurse assigned there for that day. The next day, I
was off work. The following day, I returned to work on my regular
unit. The patient in room 711 had died. I was so hurt that I could
not help her prior to her death. I truly wanted to save her life. I was
helpless. Tears came to my eyes. I immediately wanted permission
from her husband to name our child after her. Unfortunately, I
could not get in contact with her husband.

My husband and I picked another name for our baby girl, but I will
always remember the patient in room 711. I will never understand
why she felt fine under such horrible physical conditions. Perhaps
she was so heavily medicated that she was unable to notice
her own painful condition, or maybe she wanted to please me.
Perhaps she did, in fact, feel fine. It will always be a puzzle to me.
She would just say to me, "I feel fine."

THE TRUE RICHES

The true king

The true power

The true riches

The true dollar

The true blade

The true love

Death hide from me

BETWEEN MAN AND WOMAN

I desire to spend the rest of my life

with you.

I cannot conceive of being without

you.

I am subdued to you.

I have no shame.

I am not weak.

Everything I have belongs to you.

Everything you have belongs to me.

My body is yours.

Your body is mine.

I desire only you.

You and I are one.

LOOK AROUND

I just happen to look around.

I remember Grandmother talking

about her days.

She said, "During the war, I would

fix a cup of coffee, eat a biscuit, and

go sit on the front porch. I would be

as full as my neighbor, and nobody

knew what I had to eat."

I entered a coffee shop.

I had a cup of coffee because I didn't

have money to buy food.

I looked around at my neighbors in

the coffee shop.

Nobody knew that I had no food to

eat.

THE ANGELS

They are in pain.

They cry because of man's inhumanity

to man.

Children are hungry at night.

Elderly are left alone at night.

The lame has little assistance.

The blind scorned.

The deaf ignored.

The mentally ill neglected.

The malformed left alone.

The weak left lonely.

The angels cry at night.

LIFE AND DEATH

Consciously or unconsciously, we are always making life or death decisions. My best friend Mary decided that she would not have surgery because a well-known movie star had just died from the same type of surgery. Unfortunately, Mary did not take into consideration that the movie star was twice her age when she died. Mary died at the age of thirty-nine, but the movie star was seventy-eight years old at the time of her death.

Uncle Berry's mother was a diabetic at the age of fifty. She had poor circulation in her right foot, and at the age of fifty-two, her physician operated on her right foot and removed it. The circulation did not get better in her right leg, and six months later, her right leg was removed surgically. She lived to be sixty-eight years old. She learned how to use prosthesis to walk, and her quality of life was good. Uncle Berry remembered the difficulties that his mother had with diabetes, and he decided, at the age of sixty-two, that he would never have surgery if his diabetes became worse because he did not want to lose his foot or leg. He said,

"I'm never going to let my foot or leg get cut off." He had an open sore on his left great toe that was not healing. He refused to see a doctor until it was too late. He died before getting to the operating room at the age of sixty-two.

If I Were God

He said, "If I were God, I would
destroy all the evil people."

She said, "God is perfect,
all-powerful, all-forgiving, just, and
true. He does not want to hurt the
good or the bad."

He said, "If that is the case, I can do
what I want and still be forgiven."

She said, "It is not that simple. You
cannot willfully do bad and be
forgiven. So are you assuming that
you are good? That is for 'His
judgment' only."

SLOW TO ANGER, SLOW TO DIE

So you fell by the waste side.

Then you picked yourself up.

Fell again.

Fell over, and over, and over again.

Finally, you were old and weakened

with age.

So you remember little.

You say you lost more knowledge

than you remember.

Forgetful with thought.

Gait is unsteady.

Feel oppressed but not angry.

Hungry, eat but never full.

Joy, but without laughter.

Kind, but no kindness.

Slow to anger and slow to die.

How Did I Get into This Mess?

I thought that I never had a chance.

My father left at my birth.

My mother doesn't know why.

She is uneducated.

She makes little money.

My teacher is limited as to what she

can teach us as we have few books.

I eat what I can for food, and I am

thankful to get it.

Family members do not encourage

education.

I can sing, write, no one cares.

Some get more.

I get less.

I'm not recognized.

I have no future.

I must break this vicious cycle.

HOW DID I GET INTO THIS MESS?

ON SUNDAY MORNING

I was sitting on the front porch

looking at the people dressed

pretty in their dresses and suits.

They were going to church.

I thought, *Jesus, I want to go to*

church, but I don't have any good

clothes to wear. I remembered the

man who complained about not

having shoes, until he met a man

with no feet.

Then I decided to go to church

with what I had on. I walked into the

church while the preacher was

saying, "Come as you are."

Then I walked up to the

pulpit.

21

The preacher said, "Ask and you will receive." And when I got to the pulpit, tears started rolling down my cheeks, and I said to myself, "Jesus, it's been a long time."

He Said

He said, "I am sixty-seven years old.

I look and feel ninety years old."

He thought you don't look that way.

He thought you took care of

yourself.

He said, "I guess I didn't take care of

myself.

I thought I was taking care of myself.

I had given up everything, except

smoking.

I guess I have to give up smoking

too.

I don't drink anymore.

I don't think about women anymore.

I don't go out all hours of the night

anymore.

I don't gamble anymore.

I don't waste my money anymore.

I don't do anything anymore."

SHE SAID

If I had waited for you, I would have

lost thirty-seven years of my life.

I look and feel twenty years old.

I took care of myself.

I wanted us to take care of each

other.

I gave up everything bad for me.

I try to do what's best for myself and

others.

I don't go out all hours of the night

anymore.

I don't waste my money anymore.

I gave up my drinking years ago.

I guess that's life

when you get old.

WORLD WAR II

I was a young nurse.

He was not a very old man.

He was kind and gentle.

His skin had a dark complexion.

His arms, he could move without difficulty.

He could see and hear.

I lamented, "Are you in pain?"

He replied, "No, darling."

I asked, "How do you feel?"

He responded, "I am fine, how are you?"

At that moment, prior to answering

his question,

I reached out my right hand to raise

the white top sheet on his bed. As I

was going to give him a bath, I took

a deep breath.

I held my breath a few seconds.

My eyes became tearful, although I did not cry. He began to stare at me.

His brown eyes were sad. "You were in the war?" I asked.

He responded, "Yes, I was, I was hit by shrapnel."

I lamented, "Oh, I'd like to give you a bath. Do you like warm or hot water?"

He said, "I prefer warm water."

I washed his face, ears, neck, chest, arms, hands, and stomach.

I could not wash his back.

I thought to myself, he has no legs, thighs, hips, buttocks are all gone.

His intestines lie on a towel, and a damp sterile cloth was put over his intestines to keep them from drying out.

I said to him, "I will be right back."

He said, "Okay."

I said, "I want to get another sheet."

I walked out toward the door of the room; a tear fell from my left eye. I asked myself, "Why did he say he felt fine? Is he in no pain?"

I said a small prayer, "God, give me the strength to complete his care today."

I went back into his room.

WHAT IS POVERTY?

She was poor.

She said, "You need God and your

health. If you have that, you don't

need money. Money cannot buy

happiness."

She said, "It can buy things. It does

not guarantee life nor prevent death.

It can give a false sense of security."

She said, "If you don't have money

but you have wisdom from the above

and you have a measure of health,

you are not poor."

She died at the age of ninety-two years,

satisfied with life.

A MAN

I have come to believe that a man

cannot become

a man until he accepts that there is a

Supreme Being,

someone greater than he is.

Sex in the Bible

Sex in marriage between a man and a
woman.

Sex is undefiled, clean, and natural.

Sex is not allowed between a man
and woman not married.

Children are not allowed to have sex
at all.

Bestiality, sex with any animal, is not
allowed.

This will keep man and woman with
clean minds, spirit, and justice.

A PRAYER TO GOD

Dear God,

I am sick, and I am tired. I am almost ninety-three years old. I have lived my life of trouble. I have endured the pain and sorrow.

I am sick and tired of being sick and tired. I have worked since the age of eight years. I have seen two of my three children go to sleep in death: my son, at the age of thirty, from drug abuse; my younger daughter, at the age of twenty-five. She left five children for me to raise.

I raised five grandchildren. I raised a few of my great-grandchildren. I am raising some on my great-great-grandchildren. My husband went asleep in death forty years ago.

I am not alone, for you are my only friend. I have but one daughter left. She is critically ill. Her kidneys have failed. She is weak. I do not want to leave, but I cannot stand the pain of losing another child to death.

Please, Lord, release me from this pain. Take care of my child, my grandchildren, my great-grandchildren, my great-great-grandchildren, and my great-great-great-grandchildren to come.

My child will die soon. I thank you that I will go before her. You are my Lord, my one and only in my time of need. Only you can rescue me from this pain.

I thank you, God. I thank you very much.

It Doesn't Make Sense

It doesn't make sense for one human
being to do evil or hurt another
individual regardless of the reason.

It doesn't make sense for one person
to hate another person since we are
all people.

It doesn't make sense for one person
to believe himself superior to another
individual regardless of power,
money, or control.

It doesn't make sense for one
individual to ruin another
individual's reputation to further his
or her own agenda.

It doesn't make sense for one person

to kill another person for selfish

reasons.

It doesn't make sense for one person

to cause mental anguish, illness, or

disease to another person for good-for-nothing reasons.

It makes sense to love and care for

one another, no lies, no reason for

power, money, or control.

It makes sense.

We are all one and should help one

another.

It doesn't make sense that we will

destroy one another.

What type of person will you be, one that makes sense or one that doesn't make sense?

What type of person will you be, the one who makes sense or the one who doesn't make sense at all?

WHERE IS THE LOVE?

The daughter loved her great-grandmother more than her mother or grandmother. Her great-grandmother took her in once and showed her how to take care of her young body.

The great-granddaughter remembered taking sweet potato sandwiches to school for lunch, a slice of sweet potato between a biscuit cut into half, one half top and one half bottom. Once she took a fried liver sandwich. She was too embarrassed to take it to school. So she threw it in the creek on her way to school. She knew her great-grandmother loved her. If only her grandmother could love her.

Her mother loved her. She knew that her mother loved her, although her mother was an alcoholic. Her mother had gone away to jail several times before. Her mother had a violent temper. Her mother loved her own mother more than she loved her own daughter.

41

The mother would believe anything her own mother told her about her daughter. Her daughter could not speak up for herself and was not allowed to protect herself from her grandmother.

Her mother gave her money to buy herself shoes. She was barefooted. Her grandmother borrowed the money. She knew that her grandmother would never give it back to her. She would just continue to go barefooted. She didn't hate her grandmother, but she knew there was something wrong with her. She felt her grandmother didn't know any better.

Her grandmother only had a third-grade education. The mother completed the seventh grade. Her great-grandmother has better education.

The daughter was made to care for her cousins after their father killed their mother. He choked her to death and only got seven years. The daughter took care of three younger cousins, her mother's nephews, ages one to nine years old. She was only twelve years old herself.

She washed clothes, hung them on the clothesline to dry, took the dry clothes in, and ironed them. She cooked for ten people: her cousins, uncle, mother, grandmother, and grandfather. She never got an "I thank you" or "you did a good job." She never received a kiss or a hug. She attended to the children. The grandmother was the legal caregiver; therefore, she, the granddaughter, was not allowed to discipline the children. She got them ready for school, took them to school, and to the movies on the weekend. She cooked their meals.

The grandmother worked. The mother worked sometimes. So she did the best that she could. The children had no supervision. Later in life, because of no discipline, they turned to drugs and alcohol. They did not have a chance; they had a dead mother, a murderer father.

There was no love for those children. They became adult animals. For some reason, they hated the granddaughter. The granddaughter left and went away from them, but she never stopped loving them. Although she knew they hated her for no reason, she forgave them. She knew she would never see them again.

A HOME

She rented a house. She repaired the
plumbing, painted inside, put carpet
down, moved in the furniture. She
bought a refrigerator but owed two
payments on it. The loan company
kept bugging her about the payments,
so she told them to come get the
refrigerator. They did. Later, it
rained. It rained in the house. The
mortgage company refused to fix the
roof. She had to move out, but she
had nowhere to put her furniture. So
she left it there and kept paying the
rent.

Psychological

They thought eat now and be merry,

For tomorrow you do not know if

you will die.

Were they depressed, fearful,

Unknowledgeable, stupid, or just dumb

There has to be more to life than that.

ON DRUGS

Her brother went to the army.

He went overseas to a war area and

came back addicted to drugs.

He wanted to stay with his niece, but

he was so strung out, she was afraid.

So she told him she felt it best if he

went home to live with his mother.

She felt his mother could help him.

Unfortunately,

he graduated from smoking

marijuana to using the needle.

He died at the age of thirty

from kidney failure.

DIVIDED AS A FAMILY

Family. What is family?

We ate together. That's all that we

knew.

We were not supportive. We knew

no real love.

We couldn't trust one another.

Family was a place to steal from

one another without going to jail.

Family was easy prey.

They were verbally abusive to one

another.

Only my mother and grandmother

paid the bills, bought the food.

Five boys and one girl, they never

helped my mother or grandmother

but always had their hands out.

They never knew what home was.

I don't know why.

I don't blame them.

LIQUOR HOUSE

She had no education, so she ran a liquor house. I asked her to do this legally, she refused. I worked at the hospital. A lady, thirty years old, was there, dying from alcoholism.

Upon release, the doctor told her, "If you continue to drink, you will die in six months." She vowed she would not drink.

She was at my mother's liquor house. I asked Mom, "Did you sell her liquor?"

Mom said, "If she couldn't get it from me, she would get it from someone else."

I told Mom, "If she drinks, she will die in six months."

Mom didn't say anything. I couldn't understand the no feelings, but I knew Mom was an alcoholic too. The lady died in six months.

I felt that I was trying to help the community and Mom was trying to kill the community. Maybe it was not Mom but the community or the society. So much apathy, can we end this?

HIS FOOT

Necrotic tissue, gangrene of the right heel, toes missing on the left foot, he weighed 350 pounds.

He didn't seem concerned.
I felt that we in the medical field had done him an injustice.

I wanted to help but didn't have the knowledge or authority.

I asked, "What did your doctor say?"
He said, "Change the dressing every other day."
I said, "Don't you think it should be changed daily?"
He said, "No."

I called the doctor, but he never called me back.
My heart is in my hands.

THE NURSE

The nurse went to see him.

He was blind.

He had to take insulin injections, two

times a day.

The insurance company would only

pay for nurses three times a week.

Another nurse went out to do an

evaluation.

She requested a nurse two times a

day.

The insurance company refused to

pay.

The wife was trained how to give the

Shots, but she could not see well.

The nurse went out three times a

week to check the insulin dosage in

the syringe after the wife drew the

insulin up.

Sometimes she would draw up too
much and sometimes too little. The
nurse checked the wife's dosage and
corrected it.
Then the wife gave the injection.
The nurse reported this to the
agency.
The agency called the insurance
company.
They waited for the insurance
company to reply within twenty-four
hours and the patient died.
The wife blamed herself and said she
did not know correctly how to give
the injections.
She was also on insulin but refused
to take it or allowed a nurse to give it
to her.
She felt that she would also die from
an incorrect dosage.
As a health professional, what could I
say in answer to her?

THE HOUSE

It had three rooms. No paint inside or outside of it. It was near the railroad track. It had three rooms. No bathroom. A kitchen sink with running water. No floor.

She swept the ground after eating breakfast, picked up spilled trash, and put it into the trash can.

Surprisingly, they ate grits and sardines for breakfast. I could not understand. "Why grits and sardines?" I asked.

"That's all we have to eat," she stated.

I said, "Do you eat it often?"

She said, "Yes, most of the time."

I said, "I had grits, bacon, eggs, and milk this morning. I eat lunch at school, and usually, we have beans, hammocks, and corn bread for dinner or greens, fat back, and corn bread."

She said, "We may have beans with no meat and corn bread. Sometimes we eat buttermilk and corn bread for dinner. It's good when the corn bread is hot. Sometimes we eat fish with syrup and fat back grease and biscuits. Many times we have biscuit and syrup with fat back grease."

She continued, "There are times in a year we get more food, like on the holidays. New Year's Day, we ate black eye peas, corn bread, collard greens, and hog head cheese. Pigtails, feet, ears were cooked together and served over rice. For Christmas, we ate turkey, dressing, and string beans. Thanksgiving, we usually ate turkey with dressing and string beans or English peas. On the Fourth of July, we ate ribs, hot dogs, coleslaw, chicken, and potato salad."

I said, "At my house, we have, for Thanksgiving and Christmas, broiled chicken, pot roast, string beans, turkey, duck, dressing, corn bread, dinner rolls, cold sweet tea with lemon, potato pie, squash pie, fruit cake, pound cake, coconut cake, pineapple cake, pecan pie, lemon meringue pie, homemade ice cream, Jell-O with carrots or with fruit cocktail in it, homemade whipped cream, pound cake with lemon and cream cheese icing."

It's either feast or famine.

ACKNOWLEDGMENT

To family, friends, loved ones,

I would like to thank you.

<<<IMAGE>>>